God Knows Everything

written by Elaine Watson

illustrated by Judy Hand

Library of Congress Catalog Card No. 85-62950

© 1986. The STANDARD PUBLISHING Company, Cincinnati, Ohio
Division of STANDEX INTERNATIONAL Corporation. Printed in U.S.A.

God knows everything,
  and everything He can see.
He knows everything about you and me.

God knows when Linda is asleep in her bed.

He knows when Sara puts a hat on her head.

God knows that Joshua cut his knee.

He knows when Susan climbs a tree.

God knows everything,
and everything He can see.
He knows everything about you and me.

God knows that Timmy likes to eat corn.

He knows when Amy is afraid in a storm.

God knows that Chris helps his dad rake.

He knows when Jamie shares her cake.

God knows when Jeremy flies his kite.

He knows when Kathy prays each night.

God knows when Brian catches a ball.

He knows that Jessica is growing tall.

God knows everything,
  and everything
    He can see.
He knows everything
  about you and me.

God knows when Karen sets the table to eat.

He knows that Andy has new
shoes on his feet.

God knows that Michael shares
his new truck.

He knows that Gary can quack like a duck.

God knows that Jason has big brown eyes.

He knows when Kelly falls down and cries.

God knows everything about all of our lives.

He knows everything,
    and everything He can see.
Because He is God,
    and He loves you and me.